How Are Taxes Used?

UNDERSTANDING CITIZENSHIP

Gillian Clifton

CiViCS FOR THE REAL WORLD™

Rosen Classroom™

Published in 2019 by The Rosen Publishing Group, Inc.
29 East 21st Street, New York, NY 10010

Book Design: Haley Robinson
Editor: Ryan Wolf

Photo Credits: Cover RomanR/Shutterstock.com; p. 4 Syda Productions/Shutterstock.com; p. 7 Stokkete/Shutterstock.com; p. 8 ppa/Shutterstock.com; p. 11 SanchaiRat/Shutterstock.com; p. 12 didesign021/Shutterstock.com; p. 14 Monkey Business Images/Shutterstock.com.

ISBN: 9781538365458
6-pack ISBN: 9781538365465

Manufactured in the United States of America

CPSIA Compliance Information: Batch #WS18RC: For Further Information contact Rosen Publishing, New York, New York at 1-800-237-9932

Table of Contents

What Are Taxes?

Have you ever had to pay sales tax when you bought something? Have you heard adults talk about tax returns in April? Taxes are **fees** citizens pay that go to the government. There are different kinds of taxes. All of them, however, are meant to help pay for things we need as a society, such as schools and roads.

More Than One Kind

The taxes you're most likely to hear about are sales taxes, income taxes, and property taxes. A sales tax is a tax you pay when you buy something. It's a **percentage** of the item's cost. The amount of the tax and what things are taxed are different in each state. Sometimes cities and towns have sales taxes, too.

1234 5678 9012 3456
NAME

Income and Property

An income tax is a tax on the amount of money a person makes. The **federal** government and some state and local governments take income taxes. These taxes are a percentage of a person's pay.

People pay property taxes on the value of properties such as homes and land. These are usually local taxes. There are many other kinds of taxes, too.

So Many Things!

Governments use taxes to pay for many things. They use tax money to keep roads and streets in good shape. If you see people working to fix a road, taxes paid for that! Taxes go to schools, too. They pay for school buildings and teachers to help you learn. Some taxes pay for **emergency** services, such as fire departments to put out fires.

Keeping Things Running

Tax money is used to pay people in the government, such as the president and members of Congress. It pays for our military and police. It also pays for programs for people who need help paying for **medical** care.

They're not fun to pay, but taxes are important to a society. They help keep things running!

For Our Society

Taxes help pay for so many things in our country. They pay for playgrounds, parks, hospitals, and schools. They pay for roads and bridges. They also pay for people to do things such as bring you the mail, fix your street, teach you at school, and keep the government running. Can you imagine life without these things? No? That's why we pay taxes!

Glossary

emergency: An unexpected problem for which you need to act very quickly.

federal: Relating to the central government of the United States.

fee: An amount of money that must be paid.

medical: Having to do with taking care of sickness or wounds.

percentage: A part of a whole. One percent is one part out of a hundred.

Index